Out on the Porch

OUT ON THE PORCH

An Evocation in Words and Pictures ✶ *With an Introduction by Reynolds Price*

Algonquin Books of Chapel Hill
1992

Published by

Algonquin Books of Chapel Hill

Post Office Box 2225

Chapel Hill, North Carolina 27515-2225

a division of

Workman Publishing Company, Inc.

708 Broadway

New York, New York 10003

Editorial coordination by Clifton Dowell.

Design by Molly Renda.

Endsheets: Point Clear, Alabama. Page i: Tampa, Florida.

Pages ii–iii: Saint Helena Island, South Carolina. Facing: Enterprise,
Mississippi.

Library of Congress Cataloging-in-Publication Data

Out on the porch : an evocation in words and pictures / with an

introduction by Reynolds Price.

p.   cm.

ISBN 0-945575-93-9

1. Porches—Literary collections. 2. Porches—Pictorial works.

3. American literature. I. Price, Reynolds, 1928–

PS509.P65O98   1992

810.8'0355—dc20   92-1053 CIP

10 9 8 7

John Egerton Rodwell House
Macon, North Carolina, 1958

THE LOST ROOM

by Reynolds Price

The front porch thrived in American architecture from the early eighteenth century right into the 1930s and forties for one main reason—throughout the young agrarian country, largely settled by families in search of a sovereign independence, the front porch served far more purposes than an obvious escape from hot interiors, stoked by the weather and kitchen fires. In the slave-owning South and the Puritan-private north, it served for instance as a vital transition between the uncontrollable out-of-doors and the cherished interior of the home. The master's farm business, the mistress's selections of goods and produce, the home craftsman's sales, and sundry emotional negotiations of the cooler sort (with the hired man, the foreman, the slave or house servant, the distressed or disgruntled neighbor, even with the unpredictable stranger from the muddy road) could all be conducted in the civil atmosphere offered by the shade of a prominent porch, apart from the sleeping and feeding quarters and without serious risk to the family's physical and psychic core.

Yet the average literate American—especially one who's well-read in American fiction—is likely, at the mention of porches, to think first and last of a rangy white house, south of Baltimore, banked with old trees and dark green shrubs, and fronted or ringed by a broad shady porch with rocking chairs and a hanging swing that will seat at least two peaceful adults or (better yet) one drowsy adult and a much-loved child, stroked by the merest trace of a breeze and engaged in a soft-voiced dialogue of no great moment as to subject or theme, though deeply rewarding to heart and mind through a whole life's memory.

Where else in our huge national store of fictional life can we find a comparable crystallization of human feeling in a single feature of house-and-home? I haven't made a thorough search; but a brief survey of likely books fails to discover in the works of Hawthorne, Melville, Wharton, Cather, Fitzgerald, Hemingway, Bellow, Malamud or Mailer any significant parallel to the numerous porch scenes in Faulkner, Wolfe, Porter, Welty, McCullers and—though porch life suffered in the 1950s a body blow from auto pollution, air-conditioning and indoor TV—in the ongoing work of younger Southern writers where a plain front porch (a room without walls) becomes the stage for charged encounters of love or hate on the edge of a family's last refuge, its physical hearth and home.

A particular porch in Warren County, North Carolina, has been a vital place in my life, from birth well into manhood and now in green memory. The porch I knew ran the full width of a white frame one-story house built by my maternal grandfather, John Egerton Rodwell, in the 1880s and lived in still, though not by my kin. My mother was born in the house in 1905, I was born there in 1933; and until my mother's sister Ida died in 1966, it remained our spiritual home and refuge. In the earliest photograph of me, taken when I was three weeks old, I'm held in my mother's arms on the steps of that porch; and it was down those steps that, at thirty-two, I helped bear Ida's narrow coffin.

She was the second of the four Rodwell sisters and the one who'd raised my mother, at their parents' early deaths. Through my youth Ida likewise served me with boundless skill and unselfish care in all the departments of guidance, mercy, the sharing of pain and helpless laughter and the glacially slow but utterly engrossing oral transfer of family history. The account of a typical day in spring, summer or fall on that porch, at any point in my life from summer visits in the late thirties till Ida's death, will give some sense of the role and meaning of a porch in the life of a middle-class Southern family of no more than average complexity, rage or need. I'll describe, then, an ordinary late July day in 1942 when I was nine.

* * *

The first to wake in the still-warm house will be the bachelor great-uncle whom my mother and all her generation call Uncle Brother. Born on a family farm nearby early in the Civil War, Brother's stone deaf by now and sports an ivory-yellow mustache which I hate to kiss (as I must on arriving and departing, every visit). Nearly eighty, he of course wakes early—barely after daylight. Because this rambling house was crowded when his own mother died at their country home, a few miles north, he simply turned up here one morning with a single black helper and built himself a spacious room just off the kitchen, adjoining the back porch.

But once he's dressed now—in a fresh starched shirt with sleeve garters and a gold collar-pin—he quietly walks up the long center hall to the unlocked front door and steps out onto the shaded porch. His unfailing first act of every day is to stand here and read the rusty thermometer nailed to the wall. He'll study it slowly, maybe tap it twice—*No doubt about it: early as it is, it's well past eighty.* Then he'll move to the white balustrade and stare, past scraggly shrubs (they live in oak shade) out toward the Seaboard railroad tracks—the main line from Raleigh to Norfolk, five trains a day full of goods and mysterious travelers worth watching. He thinks of pausing in his private rocker till the next train stops, throws off the first mail sacks and carefully sets down a strange young woman in a picture hat—*Who on Earth is she, and why is she here?* But Brother's daily first chore calls him on. He walks with unhurried ease down the steps and heads for the well to draw the first two dark oak-buckets of dazzling water for the thirsty day.

By then my Aunt Ida and Uncle Marvin are awake and up—he shaving, she washing in their separate china bowls, then carefully dressing in fresh light clothes (she's in her late fifties; he's some years older and also deaf, though not as far gone yet as Brother). The ambient air has cooled in the night, by ten degrees; but at seven when Ida crosses the dim back hall toward the kitchen, she feels the coming heat like a meaty hand, pressing her face.

Already at the table stands Mary Lee, the black cook in a clean white apron, cutting biscuits from a fresh spread of dough. They greet one another in quiet voices, like the seasoned colleagues they've been for decades—Ida may ask if she plans to fry apples and how is her grandson. Mary Lee says the boy's cutting eye teeth and is in real misery.

Then Ida will head up the hall with a broom, out the front screen door to the empty porch, to sweep down last night's spiderwebs, the odd dead moth, and to straighten the chairs. She pays no mind to Uncle Brother's thermometer—the heat's in her bones already and her head; she's gauged it by weight, the oncoming weight of what she must forge through, here and indoors where she's spent a good four-fifths of her life and will stay till she dies. She looks to her left—the east neighbor's house, sixty yards off—and she hopes Earl Riggan will remember to pick wild berries as he promised and get them here in time for Mary Lee to make a blackberry dumpling for dinner (the midday meal here, as in old England). She descends to the yard, finds today's newspaper flung by the carrier against the biggest oak. Not even glancing at the bold headlines—Hitler is winning ground again; the Japanese are pouring their millions at the mouths of our guns—she heads back in through the day's last cool to the warming kitchen.

Marvin is already seated with his coffee. Ida hands him the paper silently, steps back to the hall and raises her kind voice to call me awake (I'm drowned deep still, in the far bedroom on the bed I was born in). Before I've made my way into shorts and splashed my face, Ida and Marvin and Uncle Brother are well into full plates of scrambled eggs, bacon and fried green apples. Each of us eats with a grateful intensity, saying little; and Mary Lee works behind us quietly, ready to serve out further portions.

But even I am ready for the day, which this early on—since there are no other children nearby—means the porch again, where Marvin will read every word of his paper; and I will sit in the wide swing, six feet from him, trying again to catch his strong profile with No. 2 pencil in my Professional Artist's Sketchbook. (A hundred yards back, Uncle Brother is hoeing weeds in the garden while Mary Lee picks the string beans, butter beans, cucumbers, squash, tomatoes and corn she'll soon start for dinner; and indoors Ida is making the beds and airing the rooms in the last surviving minutes of cool.)

Between now and noon, with cleaning and helping Mary Lee, Ida will have no time for the porch—not to rest at least, though she'll come out patiently more than once to deal with visitors—the Riggan boy with his lard bucket of plump blackberries (15¢ a quart), the sad-eyed embarrassing widow-woman (with dead gardenias pinned to her black and tattered straw hat) who'll try for the hundredth time to fit Ida with a mail-order corset, armed like a dreadnought; then the butcher's panel truck at the end of its rounds, with a few last pale blue cuts of beef laid out under gauze (no refrigeration); and Anna Thompson, our best near-neighbor with a pound of rationed coffee she's managed to find at a back-street grocer's, rare and precious as wartime bananas or leather shoes and shared with us at the retail price.

As the red column in the porch thermometer moves past ninety by half-past eleven and the air starts to sweat up close to my eyes, a pickup truck in an almost unimaginable state of repair turns slowly in and stops by the cherry tree. By then I've moved from the swing to a rocker and have been well-buried for more than an hour in my library book—R. L. Stevenson's *Weir of Hermiston*. Marvin has crossed the railroad tracks for the day's first mail and sits back beside me, reading his business letters silently with moving lips (he farms mostly cotton and deals in timber). With his dim ears, he doesn't hear the pickup; but now I touch his arm and point. He frowns hard, stands on his tall legs surprisingly fast and waits at the top of the steps, staring down.

A short lean white man, dark as walnut, in bib overalls is halfway toward us.

I know the man is his tenant farmer, Kittrel Pridgen, from up on the river; but I've never seen him like this—in a clean blue shirt, though his eyes are red as if he's been crying (I don't understand he's more than half drunk). He stops in the yard, ten feet from Marvin, and says "Mr. Drake, I need me three dollars."

Marvin stays on the top step, grim as an eagle. "For what?"

Kittrel kicks at the egg-sized rocks that pave the ground near the steps. "I reckon you know." When he looks up again, his whole face has caved in round his dry mouth, like a child a little younger than me who's badly scared by older boys and is hoping to grin. He repeats "You know—," then points on past us toward the river farm as if that explains.

Marvin scissors his way down the steps too fast.

Kittrel falls back, to miss colliding. Then he turns and starts back toward his

5

truck as Marvin's bass voice slams through the yard—"Goddamn your hide, Kit; get to *work.*" He's walking next to Kittrel now, a foot of the heavy air between them.

Then Kittrel is in the pickup truck again, with the door wired shut and the window down, before he faces out again. He's smiling crooked. "Yes sir, Mr. Drake. See, I been a little sick. My old woman, she—"

Marvin says "I'll pay for what ails her, but you get to *work.* That crop's frying in the sun this instant."

As the pickup backs out, even the parts that seemed most ready to fall at a touch look crunched in now, compacted down and as ready to last as any tank.

Marvin stands in place by the edge of the drive, watching close till the truck's out of sight. When he turns back toward the porch and me, his eyes are hot as the nighttime flares the railroad sometimes sets out beyond us, warning one train that another's bound toward it. As he takes his usual chair again, he pulls the day's first cigar from his pocket. Before he strikes the long wood-match, he faces me and says "I'm sorry you had to hear that."

Since I'm already set to be an artist, I think "I *saw* it and won't forget." But I smile and nod.

All that's left to happen this morning is the splendid smells blown out from the kitchen (all that produce, seasoned with ham; Mary Lee's blackberry roll, light as milkweed, crisp salty corncakes) and the slow half-hour I've got to sit here, peaceful, with Marvin still by me as I finish my first recognizable drawing of this kind man, my uncle by marriage, who looks even stronger now (in my mind and on my paper, in soft black pencil). Then from the back hall, the dinner bell rings at half-past twelve—welcome as snow.

The porch begins its best life, though, in late afternoon. When we've pushed back from the still-laden table at one o'clock, young as I am, I'm ready for the hour's nap I take on the wide white bed in my birthroom (already the room feels mystical to me—*I landed here; here I first saw light*). Uncle Brother disappears behind his door for whatever he does inside, in the bottomless silence he hears (he seems not to read, play solitaire or whittle;

and he smokes the acrid asthma drugstore cigarettes that, decades later, I'll learn were laced with marijuana). Ida lies on the living-room couch and reads the obituaries in the paper; then dozes, lightly snoring through the muffled thunks of Mary Lee's cleaning up in the kitchen (almost ready to end her half-day and go to her grandchild, she covers leftovers to be warmed for supper). Only Marvin reneges at the chance of rest; he heads out slowly in his black Chevrolet to check on Kittrel—did the poor jackass get himself home alive; is he dead in a ditch or drunker still and laid out now on his own porch floor, counting the wasp nests stuck to the raw-pine ceiling above him; can his oldest boy take over the crop if this proves the usual ten-day drunk, once the first drink's poured?

By half-past two I swim awake at the sounds of Ida back in the kitchen—the full glass of water she always drinks right after her nap; then a firm word or two to Brother before he leaves for the well again, then back to the garden (deaf as he is, he can always hear Ida's frail clear voice); then the sound of her feet up the hall toward the front; then her voice again, calling my name. I scrub my eyes with hands nearly damp by now in the heat and gladly move toward her. The day's deep, safe, consoling heart—for which I've waited unknowingly since yesterday, as if through decades—opens now for me when I hear the porch door creak outward as Ida goes out, whistles once at the onslaught of heat, then takes her place at the edge of the swing. The chains by which it hangs creak softly as her motion starts.

I'm still a little grogged from my nap, and the hair at the back of my neck is soaked. But I move straight toward this woman I love as much as any soul on Earth. First I sit beside her, and we swing a few short arcs in the air. Then I lie on my right side and lower my head to her narrow lap, gazing out at the carpenter bees (black and fat as balls of coal) that bumble at the eaves, remorselessly drilling their annual holes. Ida's hand steals onto my head and gradually her cool fingers scratch my scalp—not a word between us for maybe ten minutes. Then old black Pap rolls past in his ox cart and waves our way; even from the dirt road, heat trembles upward and blurs his hand like a drowning man's. The almost frozen lumbering stride of his ancient ox makes me want the thing Ida's taught me to love, the past—its sudden stark grief and hilarious grandeur. My head is still in the soft of her lap as I ask her to tell when she was a girl.

"You know every bit of that already."

"But tell it again."

"Which part?" she asks, though surely she knows.

"The night when you and your best friend tied your toes together, then went to sleep and you forgot and pulled her out."

The fact that I've just told the story doesn't stop Ida. She knows that, for me, it lives in her telling; and out it comes through the next ten minutes—infinite details of kerosene lamplight, cotton nightshirts on girls age six, the icy air, the freezing china chamber pot, their yoked cold toes, the heavy quilts, their whispered secrets on into the night; then sleep till Ida wakes to pee, slides silently up and yanks her dazed friend out on the floor.

The hours—fifty years behind us, locked in winter, though in this same house, ten yards inside—come back for me, realer than now; and Ida and I melt down into chuckling that lasts through two or three more memories till again we calm into wide swoops against the heat; and I have spacious moments to think a sentence I very much hope is true, *I'll never be gladder than this on Earth*. While I have no way at nine years old to know I'm right, I trust I am—with no doubt or fear—and fifty full years on in my life, with Ida dead near thirty years, I test the sentence and feel it again, a simple fact.

Marvin returns, still grim, from the farm—Kittrel's boy says he can handle the load while his dad dries out; he'll work his younger sister and brother—but when Ida tells him to sit down with us and cool before supper, he decides to obey. And till five-thirty we sit on, fanning lazy flies away and bearing the weight of a swelter that I, like children in general, ignore (though I see it burdens Ida). There'll be long stretches with no noise but crickets, distant cars on the hard-surface road to Weldon or Norfolk and the putter of worn-out prewar jalopies on the nearer dirt road past our door—we'll wave to each, though after a few we consult one another: *Who was that? Surely not. Well, she's put on flesh, and in this weather. Lord, how does she breathe?*

I may ask Marvin to sing me a song—an awful favorite, scary each time, is "I Know an Old Woman All Skin and Bones"—and he may oblige; or he may say

"Too hot. I'll say you a poem." And he'll reel off some fifty lines of Walter Scott's *Lady of the Lake* or a sad war ballad he learned from his father—Caswell Drake, a Confederate major, long since gone to his rocky grave, thoroughly pickled in pure white lightning (or so my mother has laughed, many times).

Then Ida may ask a chain of calm questions about the drunk tenant—*Have they got plenty food for all these children? Did his wife look bruised? Recall how badly he beat her last time?* They'll spend twenty minutes sorting the tenant family's woes, deciding Ida will ride out tomorrow when Marvin goes back (she doesn't drive) and ask for the wife; see how she's faring. Then that sad topic will fade off too; and the six o'clock train for Raleigh will stop, unloading two Negro boys in uniform—at a hundred-fifty yards' hot distance, Ida and Marvin recognize both and say their names. Then Marvin says "Won't Winnie be glad?" Old Aunt Winnie Williams—past ninety years old and paler than me (her father was white; her mother mulatto)—is great-grandmother to both strong boys and waits for them now a quarter-mile west on the ruined porch of her one-room house that barely turns rain. Silent, watching the two tall sailors, I ask myself *Will they live; will they drown in the Navy?* (and one of them will—but I ask myself this same thing often, ever since Pearl Harbor, with the joining up of so many kin and boys we know).

When the train slides on and only its pleasant odor survives, Ida stands and goes to lay out supper—she won't take help; other hands confuse her. In less than a minute, Marvin's head nods; and he takes at last the rest he's refused, an upright nap but all the sweeter. So I lie back full-length on the swing and taste the mulled odors of train smoke, clover and a million green oak leaves, bitter as gall. I know I have a whole life to live—Ida, Marvin and Brother have showed me how very long a life can be, how often it's waylaid, how it rights itself. The prospect sometimes gives me pause—*Will I know the right thing at the moment I need it?*—but not this evening, as the dusk prowls in from Mac Thornton's pasture, green beyond us in the lilac air, pegged down by cows. All I have to face, between now and bed at ten o'clock, is a cool light supper of Mary Lee's leavings plus fresh-made biscuits and new iced tea.

* * *

9

Then each one of us, with Brother again (in another fresh shirt, his day finally done, having said supper-grace in a helpless mumble), will move back out on the pitch-black porch and let the body heat of day leech from the house and our own bodies out onto the night, its billion singers—tree frogs, cicadas, the deathless crickets, the high whine of bats— and the hundred-odd, mostly decent neighbors circled beyond us, their own lights out in the hope of cool peace as sleep advances. Marvin and Ida and I will talk, again about not much but food and people who live within five miles of our chairs— though with glances at the two halves of the war, Europe and Asia (their middle son is in the Pacific). Brother will rock in total silence; and as the time moves on toward ten, even Marvin's deafness will still us all down—Ida and I won't raise our voices so he can hear—and only a final brief exchange breaks the ringing silence before we all rise.

In the early dark, when we first came out, there'd been a white moon—no sign of it now. Marvin leans far forward and hunts it above—still no sign. So he turns to Brother, whom he calls Mr. Rodwell, and raises his voice to reach the old man, "Mr. Rodwell, where on Earth is the moon?" It's an idle question to end the day.

But Uncle Brother takes it in earnest like everything else. He also leans and searches the patches of sky through leaves. Then he turns to Marvin—to Ida and me—and says with utter clarity, "I can't tell you, son. I'm a stranger here."

A baffled moment, then even he laughs; and we all join him, so genuinely, that Buck Thompson calls from his porch to our right "Who told the last joke?" (he's forty feet off, unseen as the moon).

Ida nudges me. "Tell him."

I raise my voice and say "Can't tell you, Buck. We're *strangers* here."

Buck laughs then and Anna, his pretty wife, beside him. They call "Good-night" as they hear us rise.

Twenty minutes from now, Ida and Marvin, Brother and I, Buck and Anna, the Riggans and Colemans, the Thorntons and all the dark low Negro houses between this porch and the graveyard (a dusty mile) will be far gone in private dreams of grief or shame or final reward.

All the urgent scenes of that one day, so many crucial similar scenes and lessons in my whole life and the lives I knew—not one of them could have happened indoors; still less in an open sunstruck field or the evergreen woods. That's mere hard fact, historic as any bronze Civil War soldier on his marble plinth and at least as sizable a piece of the vanished world we barely know how badly we miss.

"It has become

that time of evening..."

Lake Lure, North Carolina

It has become that time of evening when people sit on their porches, rocking gently and talking gently and watching the street and the standing up into their sphere of possession of the trees, of birds hung havens, hangars. People go by; things go by. A horse, drawing a buggy, breaking his hollow iron music on the asphalt; a loud auto; a quiet auto; people in pairs, not in a hurry, scuffling, switching their weight of aestival body, talking casually.

—from A DEATH IN THE FAMILY *by James Agee*

The Sabbath afternoon, workless, the cotton and corn growing unvexed now, the mules themselves Sabbatical and idle in the pastures, the people still in their Sunday clothes on galleries and in shady yards with glasses of lemonade or saucers of the ice cream left from dinner.

—from THE REIVERS *by William Faulkner*

No feature of the house in a southern climate can be more expressive of easy, comfortable enjoyment than a spacious veranda. The habits of southern life demand it as a place of exercise in wet weather, in the cooler seasons of the year, as well as a place of recreation and social intercourse during the fervid heats of the summer. Indeed, many southern people almost live under the shade of their verandas. It is a delightful place to take their meals, to receive their visitors and friends.

—*from* RURAL ARCHITECTURE
by Lewis Allen

The Oaks, Louisiana

In the evening when they walked about they found people sitting on the door-steps of their dwellings, in a manner not usual in a northern city; in front of some of the hotels and saloons the side walks were filled with chairs and benches—Paris fashion, said Harry—upon which people lounged in these warm spring evenings, smoking, always smoking; and the clink of glasses and of billiard balls was in the air. It was delightful.

—*from* THE GILDED AGE
by Mark Twain and Charles Dudley Warner

In the evenings in the summer when they sat on the porch, Mrs. Cope would say to the child who was reading fast to catch the last light, "Get up and look at the sunset, it's gorgeous. You ought to get up and look at it," and the child would scowl and not answer or glare up once across the lawn and two front pastures to the gray-blue sentinel line of trees and then begin to read again with no change of expression, sometimes muttering for meanness, "It looks like a fire. You better get up and smell around and see if the woods ain't on fire."

—from "A CIRCLE IN THE FIRE" *by Flannery O'Connor*

Andalusia, Flannery O'Connor's country home outside of Milledgeville, Georgia

One afternoon I found her sitting alone upon the front porch, reading.

—from BLACK BOY *by Richard Wright*

The distant point of the ridge, like the tongue of a calf, put its red lick on the sky. Mists, voids, patches of woods and naked clay, flickered like live ashes, pink and blue. A mirror that hung within the porch on the house wall began to flicker as at the striking of kitchen matches. Suddenly two chinaberry trees at the foot of the yard lit up, like roosters astrut with golden tails. Caterpillar nets shone in the pecan tree. A swollen shadow bulked underneath it, familiar in shape as Noah's Ark—a school bus.

Then as if something came sliding out of the sky, the whole tin roof of the house ran with new blue. The posts along the porch softly bloomed downward, as if chalk marks were being drawn, one more time, down a still misty slate. The house was revealed as if standing there from pure memory against a now

Holmes County, Mississippi

Pittsboro, North Carolina

moonless sky. For the length of a breath, everything stayed shadowless, as under a lifting hand, and then a passage showed, running through the house, right through the middle of it, and at the head of the passage, in the center of the front gallery, a figure was revealed, a very old lady seated in a rocking chair with head cocked, as though wild to be seen.

—*from* LOSING BATTLES
by Eudora Welty

The sun was gone, but he had left his footprints in the sky. It was the time for sitting on porches beside the road. It was the time to hear things and talk. These sitters had been tongueless, earless, eyeless conveniences all day long. Mules and other brutes had occupied their skins. But now, the sun and the bossman were gone, so the skins felt powerful and human. They became lords of sounds and lesser things. They passed nations through their mouths. They sat in judgment.

—*from* THEIR EYES WERE WATCHING GOD *by Zora Neale Hurston*

Anyone, of course, could see her, could see her eyes. If you walked up the Dixie Pike most any time of day, you'd be most like to see her resting listless-like on the railing of her porch, back propped against a post, head tilted a little forward because there was a nail in the porch post just where her head came which for some reason or other she never took the trouble to pull out. Her eyes, if it were sunset, rested idly where the sun, molten and glorious, was pouring down between the fringe of pines.

—*from* "FERN" *by Jean Toomer*

Kissimee, Florida

They would have been there on any other night, but this evening they were gathered even before the sun was completely gone. . . . For a moment nobody spoke. They sat or squatted along the veranda, invisible to one another. It was almost full dark, the departed sun a pale greenish stain in the northwestern sky. The whippoorwills had begun and fireflies winked and drifted among the trees beyond the road.

—*from* THE HAMLET *by William Faulkner*

I took Brenda Kay's hand, held it tight, and we started up the walk, moved up the three steps and onto the porch. The door was a big oak affair, stained and beautiful, with a leaded glass window I couldn't see through.

—*from* JEWEL *by Bret Lott*

The engineer strolled over to the cinder-block porch of the motel, propped his chair against the wall, and watched a construction gang flattening a hill across the valley. They were making a new expressway, he reckoned. The air throbbed with the machinery, and the floodlights over the hill spoiled the night like a cast in a black eye. He had noticed this about the South since he returned. Along the Tidewater everything was pickled and preserved and decorous. Backcountry everything was being torn down and built anew. The earth itself was transformed overnight, gouged

and filled, flattened and hilled, like a big sandpile. The whole South throbbed like a diesel.

—*from* THE LAST GENTLEMAN *by Walker Percy*

Moreland, Georgia

23

Louisville, Kentucky

While I was reading *Kidnapped* on this Saturday morning, I heard him come inside and roam from the kitchen to the pantry to the bar, to the dining room, the living room, and the sunporch, snapping his fingers. He was snapping the fingers of both hands, and shaking his head, to the record—"Li'l Liza Jane"—the sound that was beating, big and jivey, all over the house. He walked lightly, long-legged, like a soft-shoe hoofer barely in touch with the floor. When he played the drums, he played lightly, coming down soft with the steel brushes that sounded like a Slinky falling, not making the beat but just sizzling along with it. He wandered into the sunporch, unseeing; he was snapping his fingers lightly, too, as if he were feeling between them a fine layer of Mississippi silt. The big buckeyes outside the glass sunporch walls were waving.

—from AN AMERICAN CHILDHOOD *by Annie Dillard*

The Pontelliers possessed a very charming home on Esplanade Street in New Orleans. It was a large, double cottage, with a broad front veranda, whose round, fluted columns supported the sloping roof. The house was painted a dazzling white; the outside shutters, or jalousies, were green. In the yard, which was kept scrupulously neat, were flowers and plants of every description which flourishes in South Louisiana.

—from THE AWAKENING *by Kate Chopin*

Pittsboro, North Carolina

The breeze freshened, after the sun went down, and the hop and gourd vines were all astir as they clung about the little porch where Clarsie was sitting now, idle at last. The rain clouds had disappeared, and there bent over the dark, heavily wooded ridges a pale blue sky, with here and there the crystalline sparkle of a star. A halo was shimmering in the east, where the mists had gathered about the great white moon, hanging high above the mountains. Noiseless wings flitted through the dusk; now and then the bats swept by so close as to wave Clarsie's hair with the wind of their flight.

—*from* "THE 'HARNT' THAT WALKS CHILHOWEE" *by Mary Noailles Murfree*

Pittsboro, North Carolina

Jack had promised to paint the wooden swing and hang it from new chains but she liked the rusty squawks it made when she went back and forth. *Here*-is, said the swing. *Here*-is Bebe. Across the porch, Jack and Mickey bent over their poker game. Bebe rested in the swing like June Haver, tapped both feet as if they wore saddle shoes and this were a sorority porch.

—*from* THE RIVER TO PICKLE BEACH *by Doris Betts*

26

The moon was bright over the marsh that night, and I decided to walk down the road to Tee Batist's cabin and go frog-gigging with him. I was on the back porch sharpening the point of my gig with a file when I saw the flash-light wink out of the trees behind the house. I ran into the living room, my heart racing, the file still in my hand, my face evidently so alarmed that my father's mouth opened when he saw me.

"He's back. He's flashing your light in the trees," I said.

—from "THE CONVICT" *by James Lee Burke*

Lee County, Florida

Hillsborough, North Carolina

She stepped out onto the back step. It was cool. She also liked it when it was cold and she could stand there taking in the cold morning while the sky was red, and time stopped, stood still, and rested for a minute. People thought that time never stood still, except in Joshua when the sun stood still; but she knew that for a minute before sunrise when the sky began to lighten, showing dark, early clouds, there was often a pause when nothing moved, not even time, and she was always happy to be up and in that moment.

—from WALKING ACROSS EGYPT *by Clyde Edgerton*

Two galleries with fluted columns, one row above the other, ran across the main portion of the house, beyond whose gabled ends were one-story wings with little columned porches set deep into the garden. The whole air of the house was that of a retreat, a lovely and secret place, strangely formal and domestic at the same time, extravagant but never beyond taste, the product of romantic feeling and thought.

—from SO RED THE ROSE *by Stark Young*

Mobile, Alabama

29

His leg wobbly, Lucius walked out on the porch into the chilly air and bright two o'clock sun. He heard the streetcar coming behind his house. Leaping off the porch, dashing across the yard, swinging on a limb that let him down on the walk, he ran after the streetcar, but it passed the stop. He chased it half a block, and gave up.

—*from* BIJOU *by David Madden*

Ben opened the torn screen door and stepped out on the back porch. It was a cool night in the rich month of August; the sky was deeply pricked with great stars. He lighted a cigarette, holding the match with white trembling fingers. There were faint sounds from summer porches, the laughter of women, a distant throb of music at a dance. Eugene went and stood beside him: he looked up at him with wonder, exultancy, and with sadness. He prodded him half with fear, half with joy.

—*from* LOOK HOMEWARD, ANGEL *by Thomas Wolfe*

Rockers on the Wolfe porch

31

Bald Head Island, North Carolina

Wen he arrived at Beersheba, Mother and Father were sitting on the front gallery of the hotel with a group of friends. They were no doubt rocking away in the big rockers that furnished the porch, talking about the bridge hands they had held that evening, and enjoying the view of the moonlit valley below Cumberland Mountain.

—from "IN THE MIRO DISTRICT" *by Peter Taylor*

Before I went in the house, I stood there on the porch and watched him going up the road, his headlight beams jouncing off the line of oaks on either side along the drive, and I had a premonition he was heading into something, though what it was I didn't know. That's when the song came back, "they call it Stormy Monday," which by my watch it still was, though only by a minute. Some part of me wanted to go with him into Tuesday—I felt her stirring deep inside—but knowing it was just that girl in the tobacco field who liked the lonesome whistle of a freight train for a lullaby, the one who always got me into trouble, I hushed her and went in to bed.

—*from* EARLY FROM THE DANCE *by David Payne*

Cumberland County, North Carolina

Point Clear, Alabama

Dan found her alone on the screened porch that had been once, and was still called, the summer kitchen. It was open on three sides, separated from the old smokehouse on the far end by a small open space, where Raymond, Lucille's old uncle, used to slaughter chickens and ducks. The yellow brick floor was hollowed by cooks' feet where the chimney and hearth had been; Dan could imagine the heat even in this broad, airy place.

—*from* "IN A FATHER'S PLACE" *by Christopher Tilghman*

My mother usually walked up and down the *glacis*, a paved roofed-in terrace which ran the length of the house and sloped upwards to a clump of bamboos. Standing by the bamboos she had a clear view to the sea, but anyone passing could stare at her. They stared, sometimes they laughed.

—*from* WIDE SARGASSO SEA *by Jean Rhys*

Vines crawled up the screens like snakes and outdoors was a wonderful green blur. It was being inside the world. The bricks of the porch floor were powdered with the spores of the giant tree fern, the oldest sort of tree on earth.

—*from* "THE SCREENED PORCH" *by Susan Starr Richards*

35

"For years she

has painted that chair . . ."

Lake Helen, Florida

Addis, Louisiana

Virginia tosses the filter to the concrete and loosens her grip on that rocking chair, a red Kennedy rocker which she has painted so many times that she can't count. For years she has painted that chair. If she felt good, she painted it red or blue or pink; if she felt bad she painted it black. Now, she doesn't give a damn. She'd like to toss it to the side with a lot of other junk and forget about it.

—*from* TENDING TO VIRGINIA *by Jill McCorkle*

It was when my mother came out onto the sleeping porch to tell me goodnight that her trial came. The sudden silence in the double bed meant my younger brothers had both keeled over in sleep, and I in the single bed at my end of the porch would be lying electrified, waiting for this to be the night when she'd tell me what she'd promised for so long. Just as she bent to kiss me I grabbed her and asked: "Where do babies come from?"

—*from* ONE WRITER'S BEGINNINGS *by Eudora Welty*

Mobile, Alabama

He appeared upon the front porch at four o'clock, and shook hands with Father, and escorted me down to Lowe's Emporium for an ice cream Soda. I stammered and blushed, I think, and yet how I did enjoy It. How sweet and young we seem, the two of us, in Memory!

—*from* FAMILY LINEN
by Lee Smith

She walked on to the house and at the porch, stood under the light and waved with her hat to show she was safe. For a minute there was no noise but rain frogs singing out behind the creek.

—*from* A LONG AND HAPPY LIFE *by Reynolds Price*

Near Shelbyville, Kentucky

After Janey married and left, Uncle Jess and I used to sit out on the back porch after I came home from work and talk about things. This was the first time we ever did get to talk. Before, he was just somebody there. Like I was born with fingers and toes, so I was born with Uncle Jess. But one day he started talking to me. Maybe he had got tired of reading the paper and listening to the news. He couldn't work (it was understood) because of high blood pressure. In reality, he could never keep a job, but we didn't mention it.

—*from* "PRELUDE TO A PARKING LOT" *by Elizabeth Spencer*

Uncle Luden . . . had stopped drinking entirely and at night went no more a-roving. He sat with us at the dining table until the coffee grew cold and the pork dripping congealed on the plates. Then he would sit with us on the long porch to watch the night wind among the stars, to see the fanciful Cecropia moths flatten against the window screens. He refused to answer the telephone. "Peace and quiet, that's what a man wants," he said. "Whoever calls, tell them I ain't to be found."

"What if it's little old Spanky-Sue?" my father asked.

"Mm hmm." He chewed his mustache. "Tell her I have become a religious hermit and am living in a cave with an owl."

"You reckon that'll satisfy her?"

"Well," he said, "there ain't no way to *satisfy* her."

—*from* I AM ONE OF YOU FOREVER *by Fred Chappell*

Summerville, South Carolina

We'll just take you first, Governor," the photographer said, and the rest of us eased off the porch and out of range.

The photographer hid his head under the black cloth, then he popped out again all agog with an idea. "The dog," he said, "get the dog in there with you, Governor. You be petting the dog or something. Right there on the steps. It'll be swell. It will be the nuts. You be petting that dog, he's pawing up on you like he was glad to see you when you come home. See? It will be the nuts."

"Sure, the nuts," the Boss said.

Then he turned toward the old white dog, which hadn't moved a muscle since the Cadillac pulled up at the gate and was lying over to one side of the porch like a worn-out fur rug. "Here, Buck," the Boss said, and snapped his fingers.

But the dog didn't show a thing.

"Here, Buck," the Boss called.

Tom Stark prodded the dog with his toe for a little encouragement, but he might just as well have been prodding a bolster.

"Buck is gitten on," Old Man Stark said. . . .

The Boss looked at me, and I knew what I was paid to do.

"Jack," the Boss said, "get the hairy bastard up here and make him look like he was glad to see me."

—from ALL THE KING'S MEN *by Robert Penn Warren*

Mayor Cecil Faris of Tomball, Texas, V-E Day 1945

Buncombe County, North Carolina

I stir the meat, listen for noise or talk on the porch, but there is none. I look out. A lightning flash peels shadows from the yard and leaves a dark strip under the cave of the barn. I feel a scum on my skin in the still air. I take my supper to the porch.

I look down the valley to where bison used to graze before the first rails were put down. Now those rails are covered with a highway, and cars rush back and forth in the wind.

from "TRILOBITES"
by Breece D'J Pancake

Bruce found a nickel in the old washer-wringer on the front porch. The cool of morning had slowly yielded to a vertical sun; we children had busied ourselves in play that required no sweat. The day was Saturday; my father was home, resting as he seldom did in the breeze from a rotary fan, my mother busy with the endless chores that go with keeping a family clean and fed.

A nickel, shiny and fat, worth in trade a Sugar Daddy at Smith's country store that sat a long mile away on a narrow road that wound through a pine thicket. Two choices lay upon Bruce's six-year-old mind—strike out in secret

Jim Hogg County, Texas

and walk there alone and enjoy the gummy candy bar in solitude, or risk having Mama make him buy hard candy with the coin for all us children to share. Bruce swept the yard with his eyes and struck out alone as any normal child should do.

—from KEEPER OF THE MOON *by Tim McLaurin*

45

Elvis Presley's birthplace in Tupelo, Mississippi

From the grayed house came the sound of fast sad blues, decades old, scratchy—an ancient, sturdy record salvaged from attic or rummage sale. Before Thomas crossed the porch the music sped up to 78 rpm; people were laughing. They didn't hear him.

He knocked again. Louder.

A laughing woman materialized behind the rusty rump-sprung screen door, wiping her eyes with her fingers and shaking the tears away. "Sounds like mice in them cartoons," she explained.

—from "A MAN AMONG MEN" *by Mary Hood*

Monroe, Louisiana

Bethel was fitful. Day after tomorrow would be delayed, for that night her daddy did the milking.

She sat on the front porch and read her mama the psalms of David and tried to catch the harps in her mind.

She couldn't hide the cows till Thursday evening's milking.

When they didn't come home by morning, her daddy said she would have to go find them. Once she was out of his sight, she followed a straight path up Cherry Mountain.

—from "HEART LEAVES" *by Bo Ball*

Once upon a time there was a bat—a little light brown bat, the color of coffee with cream in it. He looked like a furry mouse with wings. When I'd go in and out my front door, in the daytime, I'd look up over my head and see him hanging upside down from the roof of the porch. He and the others hung there in a bunch, all snuggled together with their wings folded, fast asleep.

—from THE BAT-POET *by Randall Jarrell*

Spending the night with Tammy Lester was the high point of my whole life up to that time. She did *not* live in a trailer, as rumored, but in an old unpainted farmhouse with two boarded-up windows, settled unevenly onto cinder-block footings. A mangy dog lay up under the house. Chickens roamed the property. The porch sagged. Wispy ancient curtains blew out eerily at the upstairs windows. The whole yard was strewn with parts of things—cars, stoves, bedsprings, unimaginable machine parts rusting among the weeds. I loved it.

—from "TONGUES OF FIRE"
  by Lee Smith

When I go for a visit she lets me in at the back onto a cement porch where the washing machine leaks and she's hung a clothesline the right height to choke you.

—from "LIMITED ACCESS"
  by Annette Sanford

Robeson County, North Carolina

DeFuniak Springs, Florida

Coahoma County, Mississippi

I'll sit out on the front steps and picture her drinking the tea, and imagine that I can taste its sweetness; the coolness, and refreshment of it.

I sweat too, in the summer, even down below the sweet olive tree, sitting on the steps, but not like she does, in the oven of her upstairs room. There's no air conditioner, no ceiling fan, and late in the afternoon each day, when she takes the white lacy dress off, it is soaking wet, and we rinse it in the sink, and hang it on the porch to dry in the night breezes.

—from "THE HISTORY OF RODNEY" *by Rick Bass*

She did not know how long she contemplated the honest, unaffected girl on the porch, but long enough to fall in love with her.

—from "THE GIRL FROM CARTHAGE" *by Max Steele*

51

On the back porch I stare at the dark shapes of the saguaro that poke up like hatracks on the horizon. The black sky glitters with constellations.

—from MY FATHER'S GEISHA *by James Gordon Bennett*

Orange County, Florida

The lawns, the road, the paths all turned wild; the wide veranda caved in; the chimneys sank low in the swampy earth; storm-uprooted trees leaned against the porch; and water-snakes slithering across the strings made night-songs on the ball-room's decaying piano. It was a terrible, strange-looking hotel. But Little Sunshine stayed on; it was his rightful home, he said, for if he went away, as he had once upon a time, other voices, other rooms, voices lost and clouded, strummed his dreams.

—from OTHER VOICES, OTHER ROOMS *by Truman Capote*

It's steamy hot and the radio's loud. Fifties stuff: *shoop shoop, dee doo, waa-oo, my babee left me*. I once knew the words and sang along in a wine-cooled voice. The blues and the bop dribble my heart between them like a basketball. Here's a ballad of love. Here love is lost and much missed. A saxophone player squirts his high-rising juice out of the box.

The house is blistered white, with gables and gingerbreadish scrollwork milled by some Victorian craftsman gone deftly baroque. It is jungled-up and bug-eaten and can't be seen from the street, a residence that offers no clue to my uptown breeding. We have plenty of privacy here.

The sun has hopped off the ocean and nuzzles through the canopy of ficus leaves to brighten our breakfast on the porch stoop. For me a sweet, stringy mango and a domestic beer suffice, while Tericka picks through a bowl of protein capsules and vitamins. The kid rolls around on a blanket in the grass with a bottle in her mouth.

—*from* "HOT DAY ON THE GOLD COAST" *by Bob Shacochis*

Mobile, Alabama

Tomball, Texas

It was getting along toward dusk, and we had the store porch full. There was a checker game going and most were watching that, because Rile Blackburn had finally talked Mr. Hayes into a game. Rile had beat everybody else until they wouldn't play with him anymore and was suffering, you might say, from Alexander the Great's old complaint. So nobody noticed him come up, that boy of old man Eli Thompson's, but suddenly there he was standing behind Rile, oversized bib overalls hanging from his bare shoulders, his eyes way too big for that little pinched face following the game. He was fifteen or sixteen years old but would have been taken for no more than eleven or twelve.

—from ZIONS CAUSE
by Jim Peyton

Louisville, Kentucky

I hadn't expected Bracktown to change, and it hadn't. When I stepped off the bus, there was Mr. Deak's store right where it had always been, with the tall porch, and those concrete steps leading up to it, except the steps used to be wooden and rickety, so I guess the concrete was a change.

—from CORREGIDORA
by Gayl Jones

A black mule was tied up to the porch of the store. He had a cotton rope around his neck right under his jaw. The sun had caused the wet rope to draw up tight and the mule was gasping and choking for breath. The more he tugged the worse he made it. Two wicked boys were sitting on the edge of the porch laughing at the mule's discomfort. One was white and the other was an Indian. They were about seventeen years of age.

Rooster cut the rope with his dirk knife and the mule breathed easy again. The grateful beast wandered off shaking his head about. A cypress stump served for a step up to the porch. Rooster went up first and walked over to the two boys and kicked them off into the mud with the flat of his boot. "Call that sport, do you?" said he. They were two mighty surprised boys.

—*from* TRUE GRIT *by Charles Portis*

So the wife and I were getting to need a classier house and we rented one out in the country, a nice old mansion that dated from 1870 or so, two miles from town. Two enormous magnolias in front and a turnaround drive and a Porsche in front of it. We had dogs and four cats. We had propane gas. We had 120 acres with a pond. We had deer lice and ticks on the dogs. We had the best music from enormous speakers from three stereo units. We were working on the old wood of the house, bringing it back to its prime. Theater people had lived in here and painted the floors black. Deer and rabbits were all over the place, and I slept with the coyotes around my head. It took five hours to mow the lawn.

—from HEY JACK! *by Barry Hannah*

Coral Gables, Florida

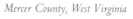
Mercer County, West Virginia

The old woman and her daughter were sitting on their front porch when Mr. Shiftlet came up their road for the first time. The old woman slid to the edge of her chair and leaned forward, shading her eyes from the piercing sunset with her hand. The daughter could not see far in front of her and continued to play with her fingers. Although the old woman lived in this desolate spot with only her daughter and she had never seen Mr. Shiftlet before, she could tell, even from a distance, that he was a tramp and no one to be afraid of.

—*from* "THE LIFE YOU SAVE MAY BE YOUR OWN" *by Flannery O'Connor*

I had been fishing for an hour and still hadn't caught anything. I was fishing for chickens. Mama wouldn't let me walk to the town pond by myself. What else was I going to fish for?

I looked back over my shoulder through the torn-out screened door and tried to see Mama in there. I said, "Mama." I was using the voice that says you're being real good and not fishing for chickens.

Mama said, "You better not be fishing for chickens, Sugar Mecklin, you going to get switched." She's got this ability.

She was out in the kitchen, that was good anyway. I put a fresh kernel on my hook and scattered shelled corn on the slick dirt yard below the porch and dusted off my hands on my white blue jeans. A hand-ful of old hens came bob-bing and clucking up to the corn and poked at it with their heads and then raised their heads up and looked around, and then started poking at it again.

I dropped the baited hook in amongst them.

—from "SUGAR AMONG THE CHICKENS" *by Lewis Nordan*

Troupe County, Georgia

The home of Marjorie Kinnan Rawlings
at Cross Creek, Florida

And even now, the house shining inside and out, roofed with good gray hand-hewn cypress shingles, the long wide screened veranda an invitation to step either inside or out, the yard in lush green grass, there is still a look of weather-worn shabbiness. It is a constant reminder that wind and rain and harsh sun and the encroaching jungle are ready at any moment to take over.

—*from* CROSS CREEK
  by Marjorie Kinnan Rawlings

The number of tourists driving by and asking after the lady writer's remains increased dramatically in the weeks after Montgomery's article came out. Uncle Billy got so aggravated with the interruptions that he began taking his chair out on the back porch, leaving Horace to direct traffic. Not every Sunday would a literary pilgrim find Elizabeth Inglish on the porch, guitar in hand, waiting for the evening train to pass through Paul Lilley's meadow, but when she was there she stared coolly past the stranger, mute, head held high, as though nothing whether trivial or profound would distract her from her reverie. Some thought she was blind, and walked back to their car to mention it to the others. And some had the impression she was a fool.

—*from* "A COUNTRY GIRL"
  by Mary Hood

Bynum, North Carolina

"A place for
family and friends . . ."

Fairhope, Alabama

Hillsborough, North Carolina

Hatteras, North Carolina

Nobody thought much about the front porch when most Americans had them and used them. The great American front porch was just there, open and sociable, an unassigned part of the house that belonged to everyone and no one, a place for family and friends to pass the time.

—from "THE FRONT PORCH" *by Davida Rochlin in* HOME, SWEET HOME, *edited by Charles W. Moore*

It was a double house, and the big open place betwixt them was roofed and floored, and sometimes the table was set there in the middle of the day, and it was a cool, comfortable place. Nothing couldn't be better. And warn't the cooking good, and just bushels of it too!

—from THE ADVENTURES OF HUCKLEBERRY FINN *by Mark Twain*

Sitting there on the porch with the Sheriff, Yasha, and Leontine, he had that overmastering impulse. He had to see the inside of the house. He looked at Leontine and knew that he had to see the upstairs. Sitting there on the porch, he shut his eyes and thought of her, walking at night, down a hot, stuffy little pine box hall upstairs. He opened his eyes, and the world swam dizzy with brightness.

—from FLOOD *by Robert Penn Warren*

The sun had reached high noon, and though the porch shaded their bodies, it shone hot on their feet and legs. A house fly buzzed around first one and then the other, to be brushed absently aside. Now and then a leaf wandered down. Faced with changes as yet undefined, the thoughts of the women turned more and more inward. All three were grateful their mother had not died, but her living would be costly from now on. If one stayed, the other two would have to pay for it.

Elmo kept politely quiet, his eyes fixed on the road. Like actors on a stage, they waited for the old man to call out and let the ending begin.

*—from "*THE CURE*" by Mary Ward Brown*

Watauga County, North Carolina

Women were sitting on the porch. One was old and stout and wore a lace cap on her white hair. Another woman, thin almost to emaciation and with black, restless eyes in a sand-colored face, sat close beside her, book in hand. On the steps below the two a wiry, middle-aged woman seemed just to have dropped down to rest. Her forehead, even the fine, brown hairs of her head, glistened with sweat. Her hands, loosely clenched, swung between her spread knees.

—*from* THE WOMEN ON THE PORCH *by Caroline Gordon*

Standing on the veranda I breathed the sweetness of the air. Cloves I could smell and cinnamon, roses and orange blossom. And an intoxicating freshness as if all this had never been breathed before.

—*from* WIDE SARGASSO SEA *by Jean Rhys*

Near Norristown, Georgia

Pinehurst, North Carolina

My grandfather and I would befuddle the eternal summer afternoons with games: chess, checkers, poker. He sat in a leather rocking chair on the open porch. By him a small table held a pitcher of water, a glass, a pint of whiskey. He drank slowly and thoughtfully. Flies strutted on his knuckles. He had a very bald head, deep green eyes, the face of Sibelius with the identical veins distent on the temples. It was a face such as the Emperor Augustus must have had: and this was how he sat, the melancholy emperor of the afternoon.

—*from* IT IS TIME, LORD
by Fred Chappell

The house, coming suddenly into view beyond the avenue of crepe myrtles, was still brilliantly lighted, the colonnade dazzling and luminous in the frame of oaks.

—*from* THE RIVER ROAD
by Frances Parkinson Keyes

Hillsborough, North Carolina

The Wilson house had a wide white porch across the front and down both sides. It was shaded by enormous oak trees and furnished with swings and wicker rockers. In the afternoons the maids would sit on the porch and other maids from around the neighborhood would come up pushing prams and strollers and the children would all play together on the porch and in the yard. Sometimes the maids fixed lemonade and the children would sell it to passersby from a little stand.

—*from "*RICH*" by Ellen Gilchrist*

He stood in the inky darkness of the water oaks and looked at his house. It was the same except that the gallery had been closed by glass louvers and a flag-pole stuck out of a second-story window. His aunts were sitting on the porch. They had moved out, television and all. He came closer and stood amid the azaleas. They were jolly and fit, were the aunts, and younger than ever. Three were watching "Strike It Rich," two were playing canasta, and one was reading *Race and Reason* and eating Whitman's Sampler.

—*from* THE LAST GENTLEMAN *by Walker Percy*

Near Cannonsburg, Kentucky

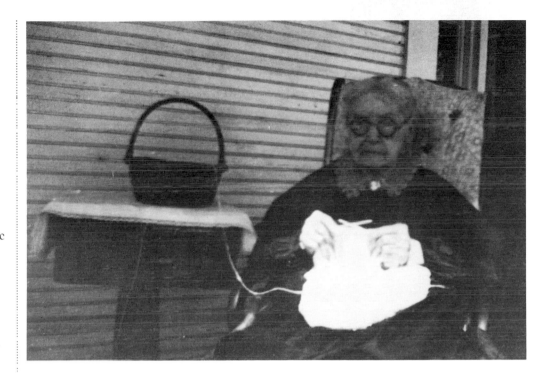

But the grouping on the porch still held, that last we looked back, posed there along the rail, quiet and obscure and never-known as passengers on a ship already embarked to sea. Their country faces were drawing in even more alike in the dusk, I thought. Their faces were like dark boxes of secrets and desires to me, but locked safely, like old-fashioned caskets for the safe conduct of jewels on a voyage.

—from "KIN"
by Eudora Welty

When I came up to the house it was the same one, the little wooden porch that looked too small for the swing that was on it, the honeysuckle bush, an old wicker rocker. And Mr. Floyd's trailer was still there, across the road, and a truck patch he must've just started. I knocked on the front, but Mama didn't hear me, so I walked around to the back. I left some avocados I'd brought her on the porch, telling myself it was so they'd get ripe, but the real reason I was thinking was Mama might feel I thought I couldn't come unless I brought something, but that was silly.

—from CORREGIDORA
by Gayl Jones

73

Aiken, South Carolina

I was sitting on Eunice Herbert's porch, over in the coolest part, behind the wooden jalousies. There was a swing there, and an electric fan on a little black iron table, and two or three black iron stands of ferns, all different kinds—her mother was crazy about them. Maybe it wasn't cooler there, but with the darkness from the closed jalousies and the smell of wet mud from the fern pots, it seemed comfortable.

—from "ONE SUMMER" *by Shirley Ann Grau*

When we pulled up in front of the Slaughters' place, Clayton disappeared from the porch swing. Again I was struck by the simple beauty of this country home—the broad yard oaks, the high-peaked center-front gable, twin rock chimneys, and the great screened front porch, lush with hanging plants and potted flowers.

—from MARBLES *by Oxford Stroud*

74

The twilight was blurred and soft. Supper was almost ready and the smell of cabbage floated to them from the open hall. All of them were together except Hazel, who had not come home from work, and Etta, who still lay sick in bed. Their Dad leaned back in a chair with his sock-feet on the banisters. Bill was on the steps with the kids. Their Mama sat on the swing fanning herself with the newspaper. Across the street a girl new in the neighborhood skated up and down the sidewalk on one roller skate. The lights on the block were just beginning to be turned on, and far away a man was calling someone.

—*from* THE HEART IS A LONELY HUNTER *by Carson McCullers*

Summerville, South Carolina

Dick walked over to the circular porch where the table was. The planking was good, tongue-and-groove disappearing under the solid base of the rail. Above it came the fancy part, doily fretwork, a pattern repeated overhead at the angle of the posts and lintel. Looked like pieces of fan coral stuck in every top corner. And all that by hand, no skil-saws, no epoxy. He didn't remember it from the war, from his childhood; he'd noticed it from afar, from his skiff.

—*from* SPARTINA
by John Casey

By the time the procession reached the house the porch was full of ladies. Matille's mother and grandmother and great-grandmother and several widowed aunts had materialized from their rooms and were standing in a circle. From a distance they looked like a great flowering shrub. The screen door was open and a wasp buzzed around their heads threatening to be caught in their hairnets.

—*from* "SUMMER, AN ELEGY" *by Ellen Gilchrist*

Mobile, Alabama

Standing alone on the porch, Beloved is smiling. But now her hand is empty. Sethe is running away from her, running, and she feels the emptiness in the hand Sethe has been holding. Now she is running into the faces of the people out there, joining them and leaving Beloved behind.

—*from* BELOVED *by Toni Morrison*

Hillsborough, North Carolina

One morning Mamzelle Aurélie stood upon her gallery, contemplating, with arms akimbo, a small band of very small children who, to all intents and purposes, might have fallen from the clouds, so unexpected and bewildering was their coming, and so unwelcome. They were the children of her nearest neighbor, Odile, who was not such a near neighbor, after all. . . . She left them crowded into the narrow strip of shade on the porch of the long, low house; the white sunlight was beating in on the white old boards; some chickens were scratching in the grass at the foot of the steps, and one had boldly mounted, and was stepping heavily, solemnly, and aimlessly across the gallery.

—*from* "REGRET" *by*
Kate Chopin

Point Clear, Alabama

Not long after school got out, Misty and I were out on the porch painting our toenails a color called Raspberry Dazzle when Merle walked by and Misty whistled. My impulse was to jump down into the shrubbery, but my toenails were all wet, and I had cotton wedged between my toes the way Mo had taught us to do. Instead I grabbed one of our fashion magazines and held it over my face. Merle stopped right there on the sidewalk like he might walk up on the porch but he didn't. "Who's that whistling?" he asked.

—*from* FERRIS BEACH *by*
Jill McCorkle

Then they tucked the old man into a beautiful room, which was the spare room, and in the night some time he got powerful thirsty and clumb out on to the porch-roof and slid down a stanchion and traded his new coat for a jug of forty-rod, and clumb back again and had a good old time; and toward daylight he crawled out again, drunk as a fiddler, and rolled off the porch and broke his left arm in two places, and was most froze to death when somebody found him after sun-up.

—*from* THE ADVENTURES
   OF HUCKLEBERRY FINN
   by Mark Twain

Tennille, Georgia

On the way over through the woods from Bryant's his horse had flushed a skunk and he stank to heaven. No sooner had he gone off to the stable than Sam and Nelson returned with the ladder. I joined them in walking across the yard to the side of the house while the other four moved noiselessly ahead in front of us to their station in the shrubbery around the front porch. The skunk stench lingered, hot in the nostrils. The two cur dogs ambled along with us beneath the ladder; their bony flanks were outlined in sharp moonlit relief, and one dragged a game leg. A faint breeze sprang up and the skunk odor was obliterated. The air was filled with the rank fragrance of mimosa.

—*from* THE CONFESSIONS OF NAT TURNER *by* William Styron

83

He wore steel taps on his heels, and in the still the click of them on the sidewalks would sound across the big front lawns and all the way up to the porches of the houses, where two ladies might be sitting behind a row of ferns. They would identify him to one another, murmuring in their fine little voices, and say it was just too bad there was nothing here for young people.

—*from* "FIRST DARK" *by Elizabeth Spencer*

As a child she always had an afternoon nap, in the old Chalmers Street house. Estelle would drive her out of the kitchen because Elizabeth insisted that Alice take a nap every day to prevent polio, and though Estelle didn't believe it made a piece of difference (Alice could tell by the way Estelle said, "Your *mama* say take a nap"—Estelle always blamed precisely), still she made sure Alice didn't sneak away from the house at naptime or hide somewhere. So Alice slept, on top of the white chenille spread, with the afternoon sun coming in the windows of the sleeping porch. Her mother was out. Estelle was downstairs, but would Estelle protect her if something happened? Her cheek was pocked by the tufts of the spread, her hair damp. It was a fitful, uneasy sleep.

—*from* DREAMS OF SLEEP
by Josephine Humphreys

Baldwin County, Alabama

Louisville, Kentucky

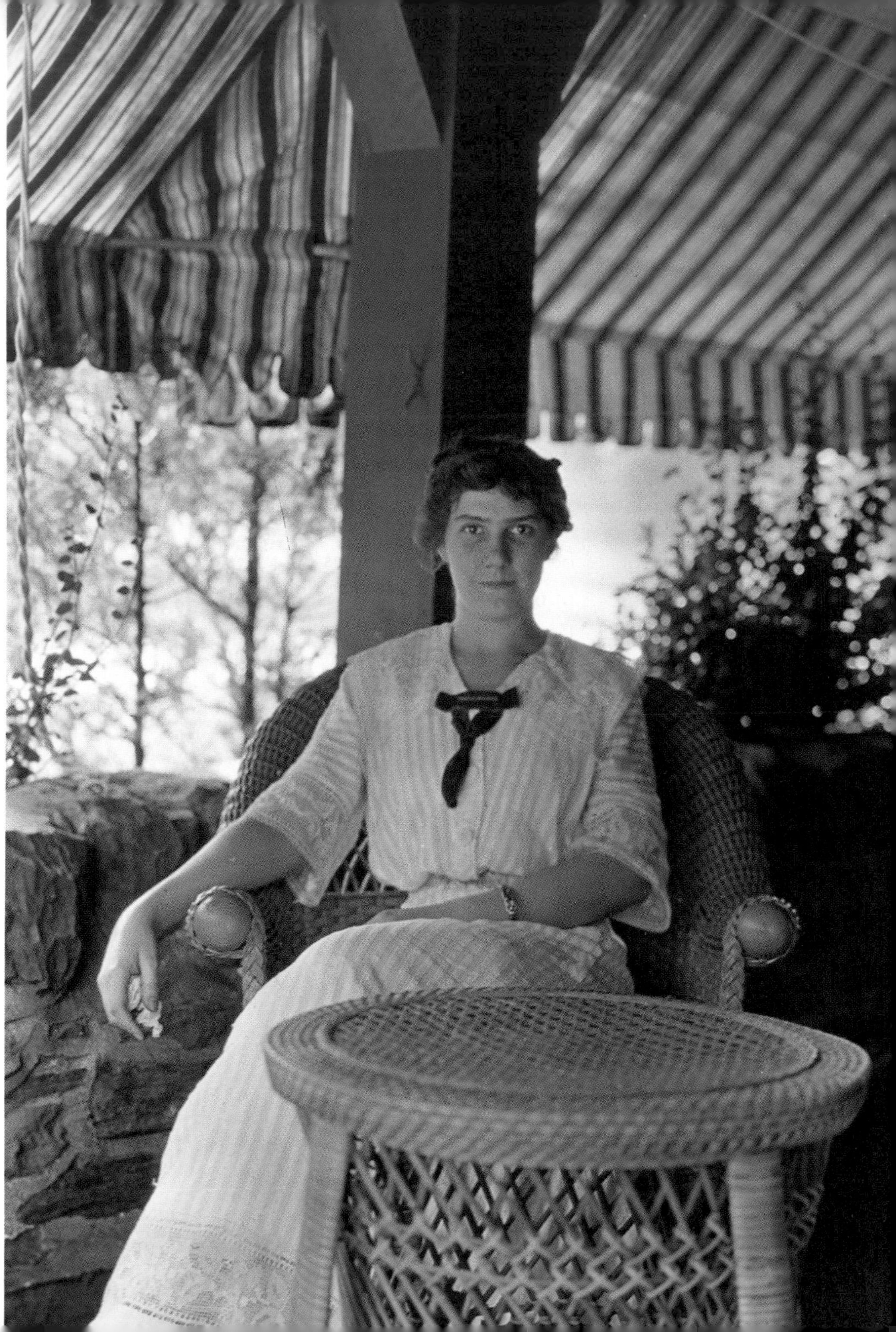

The party served one of its purposes in ways that Kate had not foreseen and did not recognize. It turned out to be one of those evenings when everything goes well. The weather was fine—a late March night, warm as May. The moon, whose help Kate had so trustingly invited, rose early, huge and red in the clear eastern sky, like a cool fairy sunset in reverse, and by eight o'clock stood, all dazzling white, high above the Anderson garden the daytime side yard. The three old laurel trees that grew in a row and screened the side porch from the morning sun cast black shadows against the house and, where the moonlight struck their dark trunks, oozing drops of sap glimmered like clear water. Moss-filled wire baskets, thick with pale green curling ferns, hung from iron hooks in the ceiling, and the washed and shining leaves still dripped occasionally into puddles of moonlit water on the floor. All the ragged edges of the untended shrubs melted and merged in the shadows of the trees, and the Spanish daggers thrust out green spikes from their impenetrable hearts. Even the bare, grassless ground under the arbor was transformed; darker shadows against the bare darkness moved in the light breeze like ghosts

Mobile County, Alabama

of lace and made leafy patterns, first on its hard surface and then, springing up as if alive, on the pale dresses of the wandering ladies.

—from A FAMILY'S AFFAIRS
by Ellen Douglas

"All life seemed

   frozen in a picture . . ."

Nags Head, North Carolina

They walked slowly to the front through aisled marbles. Sentinelled just beyond the wooden doors, the angel leered vacantly down. Jannadeau drew his great head turtlewise a little further into the protective hunch of his burly shoulders. They went out on to the porch.

The moon stood already, like its own phantom, in the clear washed skies of evening. A little boy with an empty paper-delivery bag swung lithely by, his freckled nostrils dilating pleasantly with hunger and the fancied smell of supper. He passed, and for a moment, as they stood at the porch edge, all life seemed frozen in a picture.

—*from* LOOK HOMEWARD, ANGEL *by Thomas Wolfe*

Fort Adams, Mississippi

Here I was on the porch, diddling around in a notebook and hearing the sounds of work and the changing patterns of voices inside, and the unaccustomed noise of shoeleather on the floor, because someone was dressed up for travel; and a hen thudded among dried watermelon seeds on the oak floor, looking, as they usually do, like a near-sighted professor; and down hill beyond the open field a little wind laid itself in a wall against the glistening leaves of the high forest and lay through with a long sweet granular noise of rustling water; and the hen dropped from the ledge of the porch to the turded dirt with a sodden bounce, and an involuntary cluck as her heaviness hit the ground on her sprung legs; and the long lithe little wind released the trees and was gone on, wandering the fringed earth in its affairs like a saturday schoolchild in the sun, and the leaves hung troubling in the aftermath.

—*from* LET US NOW PRAISE FAMOUS MEN *by James Agee and Walker Evans*

92

Bowling Green, Kentucky

The house was not a mansion, was not even particularly large, but it was possessed of a number of fanciful turrets and gables and ells and a great quantity of gingerbread, in the Victorian manner, and it sat far back in a dappled cave of overarching water oak trees. Great twin hydrangea bushes flanked the front porch, and the latticed side porches were hung with venerable, shaggy old wisteria vines, giving them in the late spring an incandescent lavender nimbus, a sort of enchanted purple milieu.

—*from* HOMEPLACE
by Anne Rivers Siddons

94

In summer the loafers and the paregoric sippers and the scarlet-lipped girls from the wrong side of the river seek shelter from the white sun in the shade of heavy-leafed trees, and the statue casts a long shadow to the galleries of the pale pink buildings that were old before Pelham was born. But now it is winter and the trees are skeletons, and the statue appears frozen in the light of a watery moon.

—*from* "THE GUNNER AND THE APEMAN" *by William Peden*

They sat on the porch. The porch faced east. The maple trees that had been planted around the house when it was built created a canopy of shade during the summer and now shone red as they stood full of leaves ready to drop.

—*from* THE NIGHT OF THE WEEPING WOMEN *by Lawrence Naumoff*

Bowling Green, Kentucky

95

It was a summer of
wistaria. The twilight was
full of it and of the smell
of his father's cigar as
they sat on the front
gallery after supper until
it would be time for
Quentin to start, while in
the deep shaggy lawn
below the veranda the
fireflies blew and drifted in
soft random.

—*from* ABSALOM, ABSALOM!
by William Faulkner

Tomball, Texas

She walked to the table by the stove, took a dime and walked to the door. Cary stood on the edge of the porch, and as soon as the fresh air hit her face she realized how stale the house had become during the night. She found herself looking down the path that led to the pond, thinking of the water and how she would like to go swimming. The garden in front of the house was spattered with the color of morning glories, brilliant against the green. She thought of watching them after sunset as they slowly twisted shut and how she always planned to mark one to see if the same one opened the next day but she never did.

—*from* MOSS ON THE NORTH SIDE *by Sylvia Wilkinson*

Summerville, South Carolina

Far up its hill above the river Merryoaks stood solitary and colonnaded in imperial grandeur, its windless, porticoed façade serene in shadows above an emerald sweep of lawn where reflections from the swimming pool sent dancing oblong shapes of light against the grass.

—*from* SET THIS HOUSE ON FIRE *by William Styron*

At first we lived in a small frame house with a front porch shaded by great oak trees, next door to a little girl who carried me around on her back and would one day be "Miss Mississippi" and runner-up for "Miss America." We lived with "Aunt Tish," not our aunt at all but an ancient old lady, born in the 1840s or 1850s, whom everyone, in the Southern fashion of that day, called "Aunt." It is Aunt Tish whom my uncertain memory tells me I saw first; back in some old mist a swing broke and crashed to the floor, an awful crying was to be heard at close range, and an old lady picked me up and started humming a tune. The night was still except for the katy-dids all around, going "katy-did, katy-didn't, katy-did, katy-didn't," and for some reason this collection of rusty molecules and second-hand corpuscles chose that instant to take notice of the planet.

—*from* NORTH TOWARD HOME *by Willie Morris*

Summerville, South Carolina

Late on the night that all this took place I was in bed when I heard my mother say, "Come outside, Les. Come and hear this." And I went out onto the front porch barefoot and in my underwear, where it was warm like spring, and there was a spring mist in the air. I could see the lights of the Fairfield Coach in the distance on its way up to Great Falls.

And I could hear geese, white birds in the sky, flying. They made their high-pitched sound like angry yells, and though I couldn't see them high up, it seemed to me they were everywhere. And my mother looked up and said, "Hear them?" I could smell her hair wet from the shower. "They leave with the moon," she said. "It's still half wild out here."

And I said, "I hear them," and I felt a chill come over my bare chest, and the hair stood up on my arms the way it does before a storm. And for a while we listened.

—*from "*COMMUNIST*" by Richard Ford*

Beaufort, South Carolina

They topped the rise and the white house reared its perfect symmetry before her, tall of columns, wide of verandas, flat of roof, beautiful as a woman is beautiful who is so sure of her charm that she can be generous and gracious to all.

—*from* GONE WITH THE WIND *by Margaret Mitchell*

Her bridge club met every Thursday at noon for lunch and bridge, rotating houses. This bridge club went on for years and years beyond my childhood, until its members began to die or move to Florida. It fascinated me. I loved those summer Thursdays when I was out of school and the bridge club came to our house— the fresh flowers, the silver, the pink cloths on the bridge tables which were set up for the occasion in the Florida room, the way Mama's dressing room smelled as she dressed, that wonderful mixture of loose powder (she used a big lavender puff) and cigarette smoke (Salems) and Chanel No. 5. The whole bridge club dressed to the hilt. They wore hats, patent-leather shoes, and dresses of silk shantung. The food my mama and Missie gave them was wonderful—is still, to this day, my very idea of elegance, even though it is not a menu I'd ever duplicate; and it was clear to me, even then, that the way these ladies were was a way I'd never be.

—*from* "TONGUES OF FIRE" *by Lee Smith*

Winston-Salem, North Carolina

Nine o'clock; and the September sunlight had not yet reached the porch. Perhaps it wouldn't. If the porch remained in shade all day she would speak for the kitchen. A porch without sunlight would be miserable work in winter. But then Bertha was in the kitchen. She sat down on the top step and watched the light edge gently up the walk and up the first step. It was moving in the right direction. Perhaps, after all, there was a chance that she would neither freeze to death nor have to stay in a room with Bertha. Perhaps she could, as she had planned, stay here on the porch each morning and watch the cars. She pulled the coat with its huge, capelike collar closer about her neck. She folded her dress about her legs to the top of her shoes. Then she hugged her knees and watched the sun slide up the steps.

—*from* THE GOBLINS MUST GO BAREFOOT *by Max Steele*

Baldwin County, Alabama

Dick went onto the back porch. The lawn going down to the water seemed shorter. The porch still seemed vast and high. It ran the full length of the house, swelling into circular porches at both seaward corners. The wrought-iron table was still there, white, with a thick glass top. Maybe it wasn't the same one. The telescope had been there, but Uncle Arthur had moved it up to the widow's walk the evening Dick had stayed up to help Uncle Arthur watch for submarines. And it was from the widow's walk that they watched the sky rockets on V-J Day. Then Uncle Arthur's wife died.

—*from* SPARTINA *by John Casey*

Durham, North Carolina

The hotel was getting run down then. And I don't remember the white shell road. I remember a lot of old men and women who sat around on the porch all the time. I didn't like it there. It was dull.

—*from* "THE WHITE SHELL ROAD" *by William Peden*

Her father was sitting outside on the porch swing as she drove up. He motioned her to pull into the yard under the buckeye tree. The sky had begun to lighten. The stars were gone. The air was chill, misted. He wore a woolen shirt and the hat with the feather nearly hidden in the brim. Before Jancy could get out of the car he picked up the garden hose and twisted the brass nozzle. Water streamed over the windshield. Jancy watched his wavering form as the water broke and runneled. He held the cigar between his teeth and sprayed the bumpers, the headlights, the long sides

of the car. He sprayed each tire, walking, revolving, his hand on his hip, the hat pulled low. His face was gentle and gaunt. He would get sicker. Jancy touched her eyes, her mouth. A resignation welled up like tears. He was there and then he was made of moving lines as water flew into the glass. The water stopped slowly.

—*from* "THE HEAVENLY ANIMAL" *by Jayne Anne Phillips*

Vicksburg, Mississippi

The Radley Place jutted into a sharp curve beyond our house. Walking south, one faced its porch; the sidewalk turned and ran beside the lot. The house was low, was once white with a deep front porch and green shutters, but had long ago darkened to the color of the slate-gray yard around it. Rain-rotted shingles drooped over the eaves of the veranda; oak trees kept the sun away. The remains of a picket drunkenly guarded the front yard—a "swept" yard that was never swept—where johnson grass and rabbit-tobacco grew in abundance.

—*from* TO KILL A MOCKINGBIRD *by Harper Lee*

And the very old men —some in their brushed Confederate uniforms— on the porch and the lawn, talking of Miss Emily as if she had been a contemporary of theirs, believing that they had danced with her and courted her perhaps, confusing time with its mathematical progression, as the old do, to whom all the past is not a diminishing road but, instead, a huge meadow which no winter ever quite touches, divided from them now by the narrow bottle-neck of the most recent decade of years.

—*from* "A ROSE FOR EMILY" *by William Faulkner*

Southport, North Carolina

It was a sad looking place, which for many years had not known the gentle presence of a mistress, old Monsieur Aubigny having married and buried his wife in France, and she having loved her own land too well ever to leave it. The roof came down steep and black like a cowl, reaching out beyond the wide galleries that encircled the yellow stuccoed house. Big, solemn oaks grew close to it, and their thick-leaved, far-reaching branches shadowed it like a pall.

—*from* "DÉSIRÉE'S BABY"
  by Kate Chopin

Franklin County, North Carolina

The nursing home was stranded in the country, in an old cotton field, on a square of dead grass. It was rambling and squatty with a black-shingle roof and not a leaf of shade. On the porch old women were rocking in the glare —white and black together in thin bathrobes. They watched me like birds as I climbed the steps, and the nearest one said "I can leave this minute if you find my shoes."

—*from* KATE VAIDEN *by Reynolds Price*

Where were your people from, Mr. Motes?" she asked him one afternoon when they were sitting on the porch. "I don't suppose they're alive?"

She supposed she might suppose what she pleased; he didn't disturb his doing nothing to answer her. "None of my people's alive either," she said. "All Mr. Flood's people's alive but him." She was a Mrs. Flood. "They all come here when they want a hand-out," she said, "but Mr. Flood had money. He died in the crack-up of an airplane."

After a while he said, "My people are all dead."

—*from* WISE BLOOD *by Flannery O'Connor*

Summerville, South Carolina

It was five o'clock in the afternoon Eastern Standard Time when the telephone rang in my house on Sullivans Island, South Carolina. My wife, Sallie, and I had just sat down for a drink on the porch overlooking Charleston Harbor and the Atlantic. Sallie went in to answer the telephone and I shouted, "Whoever it is, I'm not here."

—from THE PRINCE OF TIDES *by Pat Conroy*

Miami, Florida

INDEX

Lakeland, Florida

118

CREDITS

Madison County, North Carolina

Mobile, Alabama